100 facts
Seashore

Steve Parker

Consultant: Camilla de la Bedoyere

First published in 2010 by Miles Kelly Publishing Ltd
Harding's Barn, Bardfield End Green, Thaxted, Essex, CM6 3PX, UK

Copyright © Miles Kelly Publishing Ltd 2010

2 4 6 8 10 9 7 5 3 1

Editorial Director Belinda Gallagher
Art Director Jo Brewer
Editor Sarah Parkin
Assistant Editor Claire Philip
Volume Designer Joe Jones
Image Manager Liberty Newton
Indexer Gill Lee
Production Manager Elizabeth Collins
Reprographics Stephan Davis, Ian Paulyn

ISBN 978-1-84810-306-1

Printed in China

British Library Cataloguing-in-Publication Data
A catalogue record for this book is available from the British Library

ACKNOWLEDGEMENTS

The publishers would like to thank the following artists who have contributed to this book:
Mike Foster (Maltings Partnership), Ian Jackson, Andrea Morandi, Mike Saunders

All other artworks are from the Miles Kelly Artwork Bank

The publishers would like to thank the following sources for the use of their photographs:
t = top, b = bottom, l = left, r = right, bg = background
Alamy 37(t) David Lyons; 38(b) Tibor Bognar
Ardea 2–3 Steffen & Alexandra Sailer; 6–7 Bill Coster; 10(b) Mark Boulton; 16(t) Jean Paul Ferrero,
(b) Valerie Taylor; 17 John Daniels; 18–19(b) David Dixon; 22(br) John Mason; 24 Mark Boulton;
25(b) Dae Sasitorn; 26 Jean Paul Ferrero, (br) M. Watson; 27(b) Valerie Taylor; 28(t) Mark Boulton,
(b) Johan de Meester; 33(t) Jean Paul Ferrero; 40–41 Jean Paul Ferrero; 44–45 Bob Gibbons;
44(t) Thomas Dressier; 45(b) Duncan Usher; 47(t) M. Watson
Cathy Miles 12(bg)
Corbis 36(b) Choo Youn-Kong/Pool/Reuters
FLPA 35(b) D P Wilson; 37(br) ImageBroker/Imagebroker
Fotolia 8(t) Deborah Benbrook; 11(tr) Michael Siller; 22 EcoView; 27(tr) Vladimir Ovchinnikov;
31(br) Vatikaki; 40(tr) Ian Scott, (l) Maribell; 47(b) Magnum
Getty Images Cover Jamie Marshall – Tribaleye Images; 23(t) Brian J. Skerry;
42–43 Bloomberg via Getty Images; 43(t) Grant Duncan-Smith; 46–47 AFP/Getty Images
iStockphoto 11(tl) shayes17; 34(tr) nealec; 39(bl) egdigital; 41(br) igs942
Science Photo Library 43(b) Martin Bond

All other photographs are from: Digital Stock, Digital Vision, PhotoDisc

Every effort has been made to acknowledge the source and copyright holder of each picture.
Miles Kelly Publishing apologises for any unintentional errors or omissions.

Made with paper from a sustainable forest

www.mileskelly.net   info@mileskelly.net

www.factsforprojects.com

Self-publish your
children's book

buddingpress.co.uk

Contents

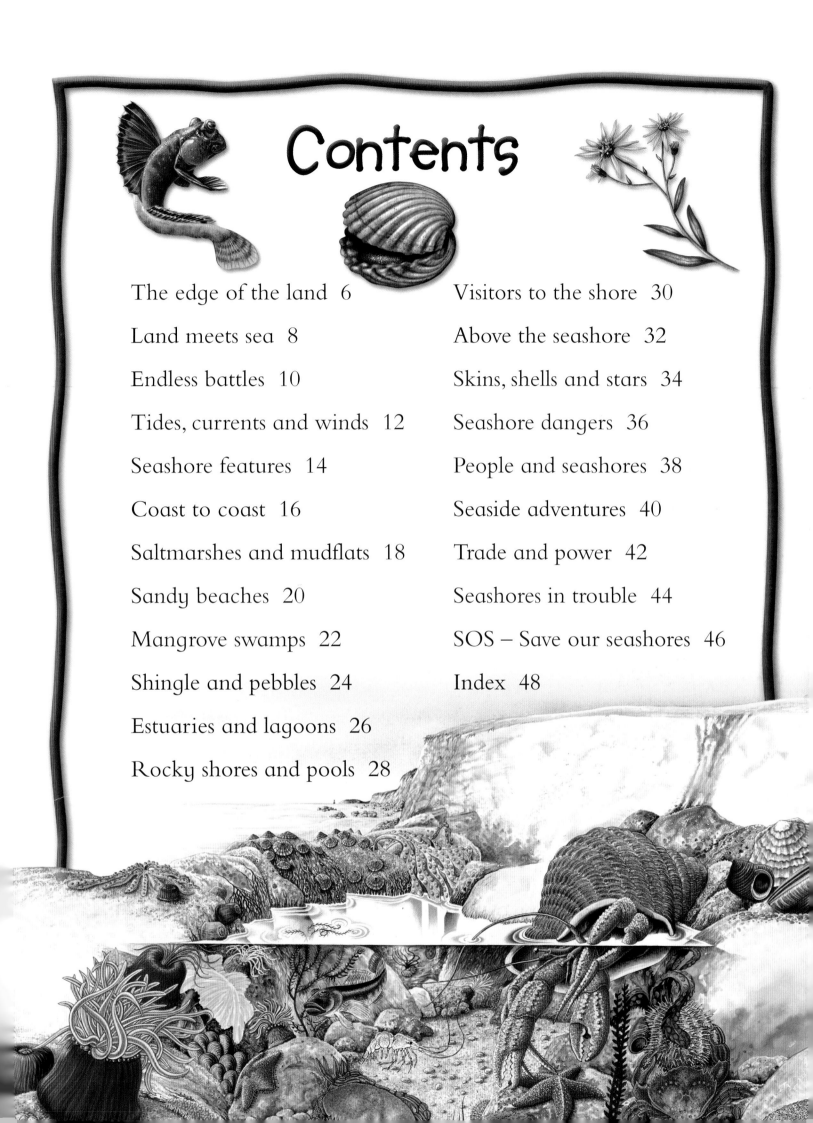

The edge of the land

1 Seashores can be found all over the world, from icy coastlines near the Poles to sandy beaches in hot, tropical areas. As well as making unique habitats (natural homes) for many plants and animals, seashores are also very important to people. Today, large areas of Earth's 700,000-plus kilometres of seashores are in danger and in need of our protection.

▼ Tall columns of rock (stacks), tidal pools, seaweeds and starfish are typical of rocky shores. This peaceful summer scene is at Second Beach near La Push, Washington State, USA.

Land meets sea

2 Seashores are places where the salty water of seas and oceans meets land made of rocks, mud, sand or other material. A seashore is the edge of the land and the edge of the sea.

Wave-shaped icebergs, Iceland

ARCTIC OCEAN

Tourist centre, Mexico

PACIFIC OCEAN

NORTH AMERICA

ATLANTIC OCEAN

3 There are names for different kinds of seashores. If the rocks are tall and upright, they are known as cliffs. If the sand is smooth and slopes gently, it is a beach. Seashores are known as oceanic coasts, or marine or sea coastlines.

Sandy shallows, Caribbean

SOUTH AMERICA

4 Water moves easily with waves, tides and currents, so seashores are never still. They are complicated habitats for nature, as only certain kinds of animals and plants can live there. Wildlife must be able to survive in the changing conditions that are typical of most seashores.

Breaking glaciers, Antarctica

SOUTHERN OCEAN

Seafront houses, Denmark

QUIZ
1. What is a seashore?
2. Why are seashores complicated habitats for nature?
3. How many kilometres of seashore are there around the world?

Answers:
1. The edge of the land and the edge of the sea 2. Because only certain kinds of animals and plants can live there 3. More than 700,000

ASIA

EUROPE

PACIFIC OCEAN

AFRICA

Great Barrier Reef, Australia

Tropical palm beach, Seychelles

OCEANIA

INDIAN OCEAN

5 There are more than 700,000 kilometres of seashore. Canada is the country with the longest total seashore, at more than 202,000 kilometres. Indonesia is next, with 55,000 kilometres of seashore.

6 Some seashores are not part of the world's main network of seas and oceans. They are the seashores around the edges of large bodies of salty water that are isolated inland, such as the Caspian Sea and the Dead Sea.

ANTARCTICA

9

Endless battles

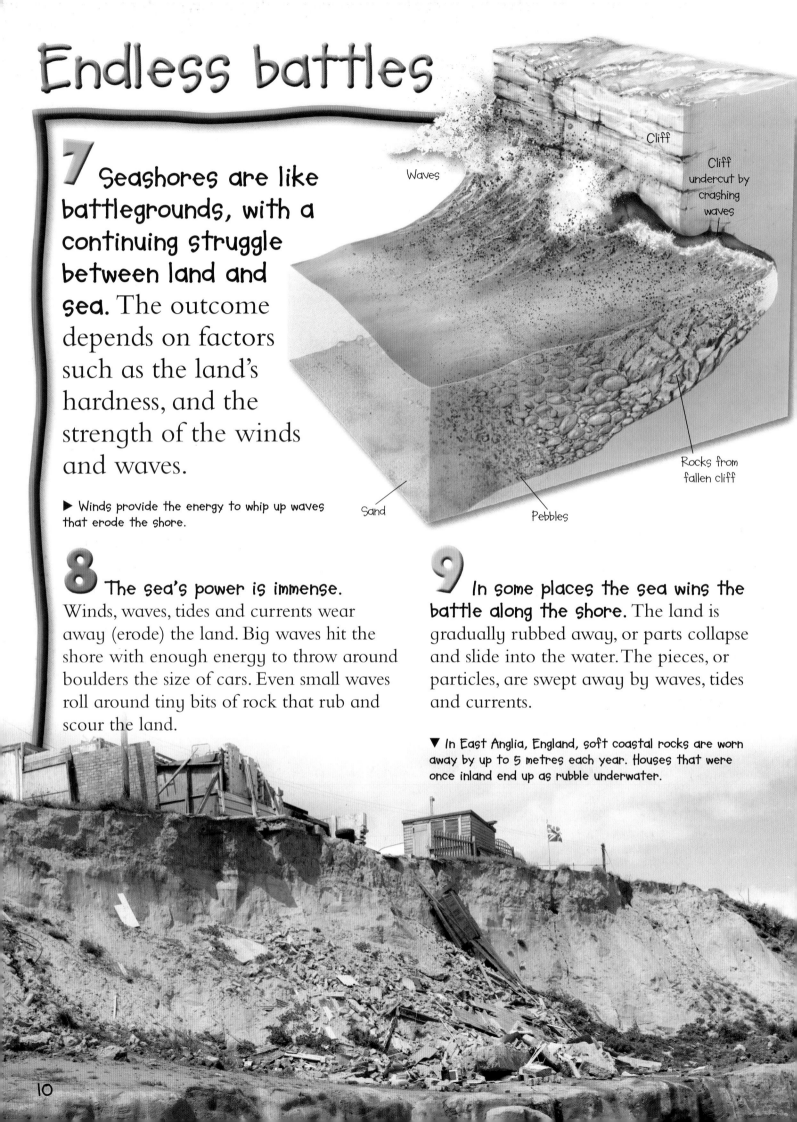

7 **Seashores are like battlegrounds, with a continuing struggle between land and sea.** The outcome depends on factors such as the land's hardness, and the strength of the winds and waves.

▶ Winds provide the energy to whip up waves that erode the shore.

Waves

Cliff

Cliff undercut by crashing waves

Rocks from fallen cliff

Sand

Pebbles

8 **The sea's power is immense.** Winds, waves, tides and currents wear away (erode) the land. Big waves hit the shore with enough energy to throw around boulders the size of cars. Even small waves roll around tiny bits of rock that rub and scour the land.

9 **In some places the sea wins the battle along the shore.** The land is gradually rubbed away, or parts collapse and slide into the water. The pieces, or particles, are swept away by waves, tides and currents.

▼ In East Anglia, England, soft coastal rocks are worn away by up to 5 metres each year. Houses that were once inland end up as rubble underwater.

▲ These granite rocks in Nova Scotia, Canada, have hardly changed for hundreds of years.

▲ Chalk cliffs in southern England are eaten away by waves, leaving piles of broken pieces at their bases.

10 How the seashore's land resists the eroding power of the sea depends on the types of rocks.
Hard rocks, such as granite, are tough and can resist erosion for centuries. Softer rocks, such as chalk and mudstone, erode several metres each year.

11 In other places, the land wins the battle.
New land can be formed from piles of particles, such as sand or silt, moved by the water from coasts elsewhere or from the deep sea. Particles sink and settle as layers, called sediments, that build up.

12 Movements in the Earth can change seashores.
Land can bend and buckle over centuries, so coasts slowly rise. Earthquakes can lift land by several metres in a few seconds. A volcano near the coast can spill its red-hot lava into the sea, where it cools as hard, new rock.

CLIFF COLLAPSE!

You will need:
large, deep tray or bowl   wet play sand   water

Make a steep cliff in the tray or bowl by piling up wetted sand on one side. Then gently pour in the water. Swish the water with your hand to make waves. Watch how they eat into the cliff and make it fall down.

▶ Lava meets the sea in Hawaii. Sea water makes volcanic lava cool suddenly in a cloud of steam.

Tides, currents and winds

13 Almost all seashores have tides, which affect the way the land is worn away. Tides alter the amount of time that a particular patch of the shore is underwater or exposed to the air, so they also affect coastal habitats and wildlife.

I DON'T BELIEVE IT!

The tidal range is the difference in height between high and low tide. In the Bay of Fundy in Canada it is 17 metres, and in parts of the Mediterranean Sea it is less than 0.3 metres.

14 Tides are caused by the pulling power or gravity of the Moon and Sun, and the daily spinning of the Earth. A high tide occurs about 12.5 hours after the previous high tide, with low tides midway between.

Moon

Spinning Earth

Tidal bulge

◄ The Moon's gravity pulls the sea into 'bulges' on the near and opposite sides, where it is high tide. Inbetween is low tide. As the Earth spins daily, the 'bulge' travels around the planet.

15 Spring tides are extra-high — the water level rises more than normal. They happen when the Moon and Sun are in line with the Earth, adding their gravities together every 14 days (two weeks). Neap tides are extra-low, when the Sun and Moon are at right angles, so their pulling strengths partly cancel each other out. A neap tide occurs seven days after a spring tide.

▼ At new Moon and full Moon, the Sun, Moon and Earth are in a straight line, causing spring tides. At the first and last quarters of the Moon, the Sun and Moon are not aligned, so neap tides occur.

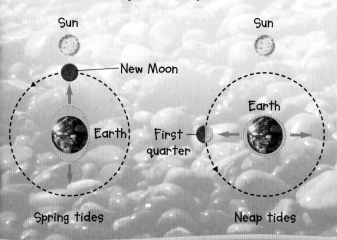

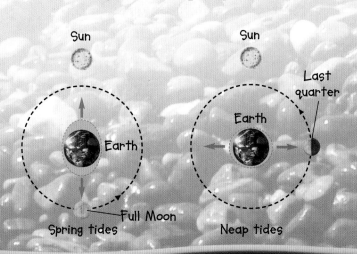

Sun — New Moon — Earth — Spring tides

Sun — First quarter — Earth — Neap tides

Sun — Earth — Full Moon — Spring tides

Sun — Last quarter — Earth — Neap tides

④ **Splash zone** has lichens, which receive wave spray

③ **Upper intertidal zone** is exposed to air most of the time – there are green wrack seaweeds and limpets

② **Mid intertidal zone** is submerged half of the time – there are mussels, barnacles, hermit crabs and brown seaweeds

① **Lower intertidal zone** is usually underwater – there are anemones, starfish, fish and red seaweeds

▲ The amount of time underwater determines which animals and plants live along a rocky shore.

16 Tides produce 'zones' along seashores, from the high tide zone to the low tide zone. Different seaweeds and animals are adapted to each zone.

17 Ocean currents affect the seashore. A current flowing towards the shore can bring particles of sediment to add to the land. A current flowing away sweeps sediment out to sea. Currents also alter the direction and power of waves.

18 If a wind blows waves at an angle onto a beach, each wave carries particles of sand upwards and sideways. When they recede, the particles roll back. Particles gradually zigzag along the shore – a process called longshore drift. Groynes built into the sea help to control it, so beaches don't wash away.

Seashore features

19 On a typical seashore, the struggle between land and sea produces various features. Much depends on the balance between the sea's wearing away of the land, and the formation of new land by particles settling in layers, known as sedimentation.

Headland

Stack

Arch

Stump

Needle

20 Hard or tough rocks can resist the sea's eroding power. They form tall cliffs and headlands that erode slowly. Softer rocks break apart more easily. The waves erode them at sea level, which is known as undercutting. The whole shore collapses as boulders tumble into the water.

Shingle spit

21 Waves and other shore-eroding forces may gradually cut through a headland, forming a cave. This can get worn through to form an arch of rock. When the arch collapses it leaves an isolated tall piece of rock, called a stack.

Shingle or pebble beach

Groyne

▲ In this bay, waves and currents wash sediments with increasing power from right to left. Wall-like groynes or breakwaters lessen longshore drift.

Circular bay

Cave

Waves

Cliffs

22 Waves and onshore currents flowing towards the land bring sediments to make low shores and mounds of sand, mud and silt. These can lengthen to form long spits. During extra-high spring tides these sediments grow higher.

River →

23 Depending on winds and currents, a huge rounded scoop may be carved along the seashore to form a bay. In sheltered parts of the bay, particles of sand gather to form a beach. As the bay gets more curved, it can break through the land behind to leave an island.

Delta

Mudflats (bare mud near delta)

Saltmarsh (with plants)

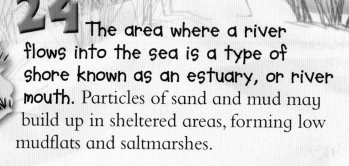

Sandy beach

24 The area where a river flows into the sea is a type of shore known as an estuary, or river mouth. Particles of sand and mud may build up in sheltered areas, forming low mudflats and saltmarshes.

Coast to coast

25 A seashore's features and wildlife depend on its location. Seashores near the Poles are cold most of the year and the sea may freeze for months. Almost no life can survive there.

◀ Antarctic coasts are mostly floating sheets and lumps of ice. Crabeater seals rest at the ice edge after feeding in the almost freezing water.

26 Some cold seashores have no land. Glaciers and ice shelves spread outwards, so the sea meets ice, not land. The edge of the ice may have smooth slopes and platforms cut by the waves. Jagged chunks of ice crack off and fall into the water as floating icebergs.

▼ Tropical seashores include coral reefs, like this one near Komodo Island, Southeast Asia, with huge biodiversity (range of living things).

27 In tropical regions around the middle of the Earth, seashore conditions are very different. It is warm for most of the year and many forms of life flourish, including seaweeds, fish, crabs, prawns, starfish and corals.

28 Exposure to wind is a powerful factor in the shaping of a shoreline. A windward seashore is exposed to strong prevailing winds. The winds make waves that hit the shore hard, sending salty spray to great heights. This type of shore has very different animals and plants from a leeward seashore, which is sheltered from the main winds.

29 Yearly seasons have an effect on seashores and their wildlife. Usually there is rough weather in winter, with winds and storms that increase land erosion. Some wildlife moves away from the shore in winter – birds fly inland while lobsters and fish move into deeper water.

30 The slope of the sea bed at the shore is very important, affecting the size and number of waves. A sea bed with a very shallow slope tends to produce smaller waves. A steep slope up to the beach gives bigger waves that erode the land faster, but are good for surfing!

LET'S SURF!
You will need:
sink or bathtub   water   tray
Put 10 centimetres of water into the sink or bathtub. Hold the tray at one end, at an angle so that part of it slopes into the water like a beach. Swish your other hand in the water to make waves hit the 'beach'. How does altering the tray's angle from low to high affect the waves?

▲ A big winter storm, such as this one in Sussex, UK, can smash even the strongest sea defences, which have to be repaired regularly.

Saltmarshes and mudflats

Sea thrift (sea pink) likes drier areas of marsh

Common cordgrass helps bind loose mud

Glasswort has fleshy leaves that store water

Sea aster flowers in late summer

▲ Saltmarsh plants have to endure harsh conditions, as they are exposed to both salt water and freshwater.

31 On a sheltered seashore, small particles of sediment collect. This happens around the mouths of rivers (estuaries). As the river's water speed slows, its floating particles sink to the bottom.

32 Saltmarshes have partly dry areas. They are rarely fully submerged, perhaps only with salty water at spring tides, or with freshwater if a nearby river floods.

▶ Many wading birds feed by probing into mud for small worms and shellfish.

Redshank

Curlew

33 Saltmarsh plants include glasswort, sea purslane, sea aster, sea lavender, sea thrift and red fescue. These plants are food for small creatures such as worms and insects, which are eaten by birds such as rails, curlews, herons and egrets.

34 Mudflats are usually lower and wetter than saltmarshes, as every high tide washes over them. Plants find it difficult to take root in these conditions, but a few, such as rice grass, cordgrass and eel grass, manage. Cordgrass grows in the wetter regions of saltmarshes around the world. It has glands to get rid of unwanted salt taken in from sea water.

35 Most mudflat animal life is under the surface. There are burrowing animals such as ragworms, mud shrimps and ghost crabs, and shelled creatures such as spireshells, towershells, cockles and various types of clams. Birds, especially waders such as godwits, knots and snipes, fly in at low tide to probe for these creatures.

Soft-shell clams like muddy shores best

Laver spireshells are also called mudsnails

Towershells feed in both sand and silt

Common cockles filter sea water for food

▲ Shelled animals with two shell halves are called bivalves. Spiral ones are types of sea-snails.

▼ Each year, summer plants grow into the calm waters of saltmarshes, spreading their greenery into the channels. However autumn storms soon wash them away.

I DON'T BELIEVE IT!

In some mudflats, the numbers of small shellfish, called spireshells, are greater than 50,000 in just one square metre!

Sandy beaches

36 Sandy shores need gentle winds, waves and currents that are still strong enough to wash away silt and mud. Just above high tide, any rain quickly drains away between the grains of sand, so it is too dry for land plants to grow. Below this, the grains move with wind, waves and tides, so few sea plants can grow there either.

37 Most sandy shore life is under the surface. Animals hide under the sand while the tide is out. As it rises, it brings with it tiny plants and animals, known as plankton, and bits of dead plants and creatures. Shrimps, lugworms, clams, tellins, scallops and heart urchins burrow through the sand or filter the water to feed.

38 Small sandy shore animals are meals for bigger predators that follow the tide, including cuttlefish, octopus and fish such as sea bass and flatfish. The giant sea bass of North Pacific shores grows to more than 2 metres long and weighs 250 kilograms.

▼ As the tide comes in, creatures hidden in the sand come out and start to feed — but predators are ready to eat them.

Jellyfish may get washed up onto the beach and stranded

Cuttlefish grab prey with their tentacles

Sand eels feed on the bottom

Flatfish have colours similar to the sea bed

Common shrimps half-hide in burrows

▼ Fencing helps to keep sand dunes still, so grasses can start to grow.

39 As high tide retreats, it leaves a ribbon of washed-up debris along a beach, called the **strandline.** Animals including gulls, foxes, otters and lizards scavenge here for food, such as dead fish and crabs.

40 On some sandy shores, onshore winds blow the sand grains up the beach towards the land. Mounds, ridges and hills form seashore habitats called sand dunes. Marram grass can survive the wind and dryness, and its roots stop the grains blowing away, stabilizing the dunes.

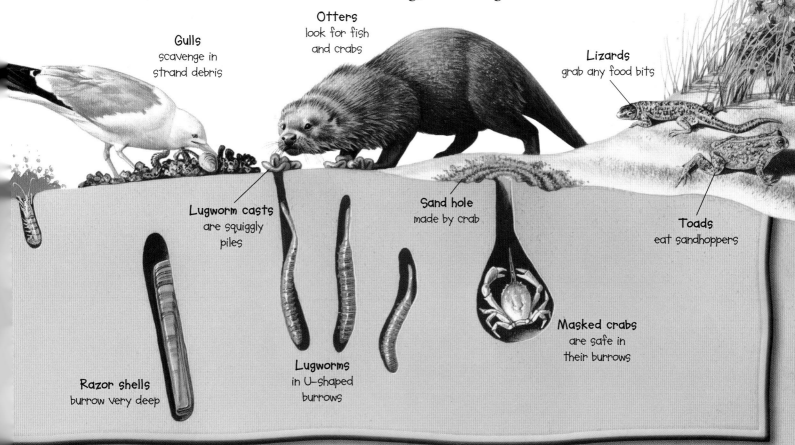

Gulls
scavenge in
strand debris

Otters
look for fish
and crabs

Lizards
grab any food bits

Lugworm casts
are squiggly
piles

Sand hole
made by crab

Toads
eat sandhoppers

Razor shells
burrow very deep

Lugworms
in U-shaped
burrows

Masked crabs
are safe in
their burrows

Mangrove swamps

41 **Mangrove swamps are unusual shore habitats.** They occur in the tropics where wind, waves and currents are weak, allowing mud to collect. The mud has no tiny air pockets, which land plants need to take oxygen from.

◄ Shoreline mangroves, here in East Africa, form a thick tangle where no other plants grow. These mangrove trees have stilt roots.

42 **Mangrove trees use their unusual roots to get oxygen from the air.** Some have stilt or prop roots, which hold the tree above the mud and water so it can take in oxygen through tiny holes in its bark. Others have aerial roots covered with tiny holes that poke above the mud into the air.

▼ Black mangroves, like these in Florida, USA, have aerial roots covered with tiny holes that poke above the mud into the air.

43 **Mangrove swamps teem with wildlife.** The biggest creatures include dugongs and manatees (large marine mammals) that eat the fallen leaves, flowers and fruits of mangrove trees. Fish and turtles swim among the roots, while mangrove and fiddler crabs burrow in the mud or climb the roots.

▲ Mangrove roots, stems and seaweeds form an underwater jungle where small predators, such as this lemon shark pup, hunt for victims.

44 **Roosting birds, land crabs, mangrove snakes and fishing cats live in mangroves.** In South and Southeast Asia, tigers slink between the trees looking for prey. One of the strangest inhabitants is the proboscis monkey. The male has a long, floppy nose, which can be up to 8 centimetres in length.

Male proboscis monkey

Female proboscis monkey

► Proboscis monkeys eat mainly mangrove leaves and fruits, and they are excellent swimmers.

Baby proboscis monkey

Shingle and pebbles

45 One of the harshest seashore habitats is the shingle, pebble or gravel beach. Fairly strong winds, waves and currents wash away smaller particles, such as silt and sand, leaving behind lumps of rock and stone. Sand or mud may collect over time, but a strong storm's crashing waves wash them away.

◀ On this New Zealand shingle beach, a storm has washed away some of the smaller pebbles to leave a line of larger cobbles, which protect the shingle higher up.

HIDDEN EGGS

You will need:
smooth, rounded pebbles   tray
watercolour paints and brush
three hen's eggs

Lay out the pebbles on the tray and look at their colours and patterns. Paint the hen's eggs to match the pebbles. Place the eggs among the pebbles. Are they so well camouflaged that your friends can't spot them?

46 Waves roll shingle and pebbles around, wearing away their sharp edges and making them smooth and rounded. Plants are in danger of being crushed by the waves, but oysterplant, sea kale and sea blite gain a roothold. Lichens, combinations of fungi or moulds, and simple plants known as algae, coat the stones.

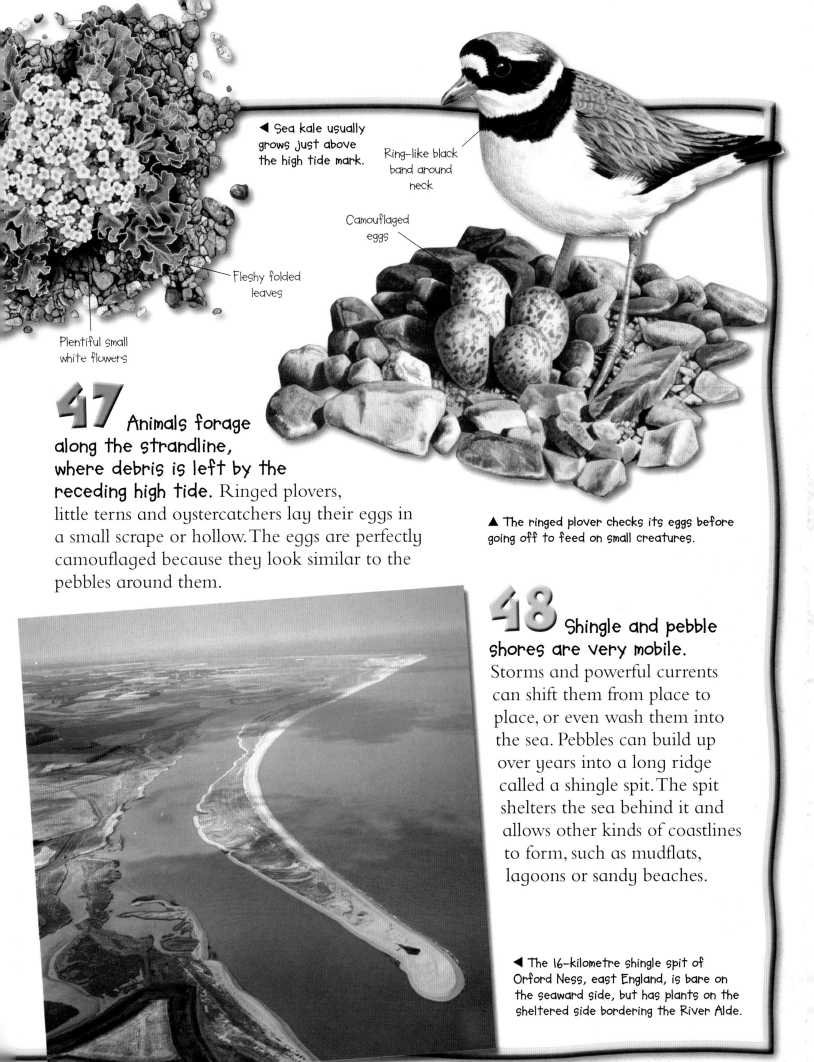

◄ Sea kale usually grows just above the high tide mark.

Ring-like black band around neck

Camouflaged eggs

Fleshy folded leaves

Plentiful small white flowers

47 Animals forage along the strandline, where debris is left by the receding high tide. Ringed plovers, little terns and oystercatchers lay their eggs in a small scrape or hollow. The eggs are perfectly camouflaged because they look similar to the pebbles around them.

▲ The ringed plover checks its eggs before going off to feed on small creatures.

48 Shingle and pebble shores are very mobile. Storms and powerful currents can shift them from place to place, or even wash them into the sea. Pebbles can build up over years into a long ridge called a shingle spit. The spit shelters the sea behind it and allows other kinds of coastlines to form, such as mudflats, lagoons or sandy beaches.

◄ The 16-kilometre shingle spit of Orford Ness, east England, is bare on the seaward side, but has plants on the sheltered side bordering the River Alde.

Estuaries and lagoons

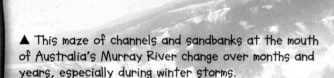

▲ This maze of channels and sandbanks at the mouth of Australia's Murray River change over months and years, especially during winter storms.

49 **An estuary is the end of a river at the coast, where it flows into the sea.** The river might emerge through a narrow gap. Or it can gradually widen as it approaches the sea, so that at the shore it is so wide you cannot see from one side to the other.

50 **The river water slows down as it flows into the sea and loses its movement energy.** As this happens, its sediment particles settle out in order of size. This is known as sediment sorting or grading. As particles settle to the bottom, they may form a spreading area in the river mouth called a delta.

51 **Estuaries are halfway habitats, with freshwater towards the river and salt water towards the sea.** There is an ever-changing mixture inbetween due to tides, currents and rainfall. This partly salty water is known as brackish.

▶ Grizzly bears dig up tasty shellfish on an estuary beach in Canada.

▶ This circular island in the Maldives, called a coral atoll, has a lagoon in the middle.

52 A lagoon is a sheltered area behind some kind of barrier, such as a ridge of shingle or a coral reef. Protected from the full force of the waves, lagoons are usually calm, warm, shallow and full of life.

▼ Blacktip reef sharks often gather in shallow lagoons and estuaries in the breeding season to find partners and mate. They lay eggs here, where the baby sharks are safer from large predators than in the open water.

53 The tallest inhabitants in some coastal lagoons are flamingos, such as the American and greater flamingo. They filter tiny shrimps, shellfish and plants from the water with the brush-like bristles inside their beaks.

Rocky shores and pools

54 Where the land is made from hard rock, different kinds of rocky shores form. They vary with the rock's hardness, the size of the pieces, and whether the shore is exposed to wind, waves and currents. Tidal zones (see page 13) are usually visible on these shores with 'lines' of seaweeds.

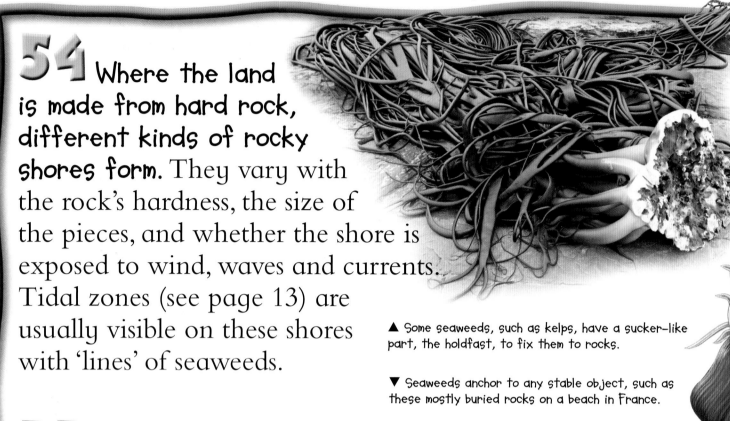

▲ Some seaweeds, such as kelps, have a sucker-like part, the holdfast, to fix them to rocks.

▼ Seaweeds anchor to any stable object, such as these mostly buried rocks on a beach in France.

55 Channelled wrack, a green seaweed, often grows high on the shore with bladderwrack. Knotted rack grows slightly lower. Towards the low tide area are brown seaweeds, such as oarweeds and kelps, and even lower are red seaweeds. These plants vary depending on the coast's exposure to wind and waves.

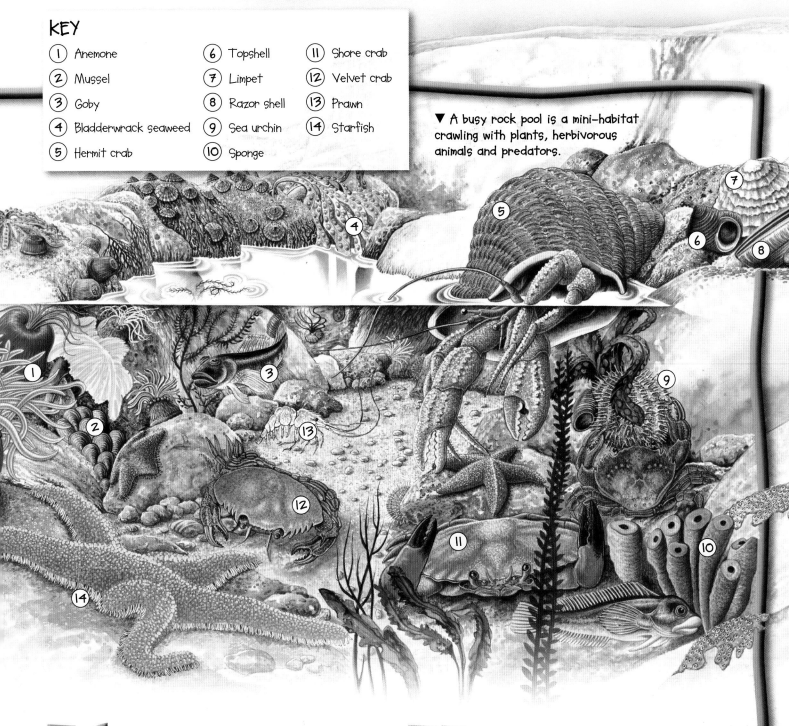

KEY
1 Anemone
2 Mussel
3 Goby
4 Bladderwrack seaweed
5 Hermit crab
6 Topshell
7 Limpet
8 Razor shell
9 Sea urchin
10 Sponge
11 Shore crab
12 Velvet crab
13 Prawn
14 Starfish

▼ A busy rock pool is a mini-habitat crawling with plants, herbivorous animals and predators.

56 Fixed-down creatures such as barnacles and mussels live on the bare rocks of the mid-tidal zones. As the tide comes in they filter tiny edible particles from the water. Limpets hold onto the rocks firmly and move slowly, scraping off plant growth. Seaweeds form forests for smaller animals such as shellfish, crabs, prawns, and fish such as gobies and blennies, as well as starfish, anemones, sea mats and sea squirts.

57 Seashore rock pools are left behind as the tide retreats. They are miniature communities of animals and plants. The seaweeds capture the Sun's light energy for growth. Herbivorous animals such as periwinkles and limpets eat the plants. Predators ranging from whelks to octopus hide among the crevices and prey on the herbivores.

Visitors to the shore

58 **Many animals visit seashores.** Some of them come to feed or breed. Others stop there to rest during long journeys or to escape danger such as predators or harsh conditions inland or out at sea. Otters like to catch fish and crabs in the pools and shallows.

▲ Sea lion pups may feed on their mother's milk for up to one year.

◄ Male Southern elephant seals roar and fight rivals on the beach. Winners get to mate with females.

59 **Seals, sea lions and walruses are ideally suited to diving, swimming and feeding at sea.** But they come ashore to beaches or rocks to rest and sunbathe.

60 **Seals and sea lions have their young (pups) along the seashore.** The pups feed on their mothers' milk, then stay ashore while the mothers return to the sea to catch food. Within two or three weeks the pups can swim and dive.

▲ Terns flock down to rest overnight on a remote
beach before continuing their migration.

61 Visiting birds use seashores as resting places on their long yearly journeys (migrations). Some move to the coast for winter, when inland waters freeze. Migrants include waders or shorebirds such as dunlins, sandpipers, godwits and curlews. Wildfowl such as ducks, geese and swans also stop over on migration or overwinter on the shore.

▶ After laying about 150 eggs into the hole she dug, this female green turtle pushes sand on top to close the hole before returning to the water.

62 Among the rarest shore visitors is the sea turtle. The female hauls herself up the beach under cover of darkness, scoops a large hole with her flippers, lays her eggs in it, covers them and lumbers back to the sea. Weeks later the baby turtles hatch and dig their way to the surface. Then it's a race to the sea – many will be eaten by gathering predators on the way.

31

Above the seashore

63 The skies above many seashores are busy with all kinds of flying animals. Several kinds of birds rest or nest along the shore, flying out to sea or inland to feed.

◀ Different kinds of birds tend to perch and nest at different heights along the cliffs.

64 Coastal cliffs are safe nesting places for many different seabirds. It is difficult for predators, such as foxes, lizards or snakes, to reach the birds' eggs and chicks on steep rocky ledges. Cliff-nesters include fulmars, puffins, Manx shearwaters and gannets.

KEY

1. Great black-backed gull
2. Lesser black-backed gull
3. Herring gull
4. Rock dove
5. Chough
6. Puffin
7. Guillemot
8. Razorbill
9. Rock pipit
10. Fulmar
11. Kittiwake
12. Black guillemot

66 As darkness falls along the shore, most birds settle to rest. The nocturnal (night-time) fliers such as owls and bats come out. The coastal sheath-tail bat of Australia and Papua New Guinea feeds mainly on beetles and other insects. Along the shores of southwest North America, the fishing bat swoops down to catch fish, crabs and other creatures.

▲ The caracara, a type of falcon, pecks the flesh from mussels.

65 Some birds fly along coasts when looking for food, including gulls, waders, wildfowl and birds of prey. There are several types of sea eagle, including the bald eagle (national emblem of the USA) and the even more powerful Steller's sea eagle.

67 Flying insects are also common along seashores, especially in the summer. Beetles and flies buzz around washed-up rotting seaweeds, fish and other debris. Butterflies flutter along the upper shore and cliffs, searching for sweet nectar in the flowers. They include the bitterbush blue butterfly of Australia, and North America's rare Lange's metalmark butterfly, which inhabits sand dunes.

I DON'T BELIEVE IT!

The peregrine falcon hunts along the shore as well as inland. It kills other birds by power-diving onto them at speeds of more than 200 kilometres an hour, making it the world's fastest animal.

▶ Grayling butterflies sunbathe on sea holly and shore rocks.

Sea holly

Skins, shells and stars

68 Many kinds of small seashore fish, such as gobies, shannies and blennies, don't have scales. They are covered in tough, smooth, slippery skin. This helps them to wriggle through seaweed and slip away from rolling pebbles.

▲ The soft-bodied hermit crab uses an empty sea-snail shell for protection, finding a larger one as it grows.

▼ Mudskippers can stay out of water for several hours and 'skip' on their front fins.

69 Crabs scuttle and swim across the shore. They have eight walking legs and two strong pincers (chelae). Many are scavengers, eating whatever they can find. Others hunt small fish and similar creatures. Their long-bodied cousins are lobsters, which grow to one metre long.

FISHY FACTS!

You will need:
notebook   pen

Next time you're in a supermarket or fishmonger, look for the various kinds of fish and shellfish on sale – cod, salmon, prawns, mussels and so on. Make a list of them. Do some research and find out which ones live along seashores – probably quite a few!

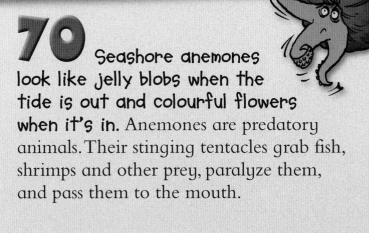

70 Seashore anemones look like jelly blobs when the tide is out and colourful flowers when it's in. Anemones are predatory animals. Their stinging tentacles grab fish, shrimps and other prey, paralyze them, and pass them to the mouth.

71 Starfish are slow but deadly hunters. They grab shellfish such as mussels, and gradually pull their shell halves apart. The starfish then turns its stomach inside out through its mouth, and pushes this through the gap between the shell halves to digest the flesh within.

▼ The scallop snaps its two shell valves shut, creating a jet of water that pushes it away from danger, such as a hungry starfish.

72 Shellfish abound on the seashore. Whelks and topshells have snail-like curly shells. Cowries have beautifully patterned shells in bright colours. Bivalve shellfish such as clams, oysters, cockles and scallops have two halves (valves) to the shell.

▶ Goose barnacles are related to crabs. Their feathery feeding tentacles filter tiny bits of food from sea water.

35

Seashore dangers

73 Seashores can be hit by many types of natural disasters. Among the most deadly are giant waves called tsunamis. These are usually set off by underwater earthquakes, volcanoes or landslides, which shake the sea bed and push water into massive ripples that spread out until they reach a shore.

③ Wave gets taller but slower as it approaches the coast

② An upward wave is formed

④ Wave crashes or breaks onto the coast

① Undersea earthquake moves large amount of water

▲ As tsunami waves enter shallow water, they move more slowly but grow taller.

74 The high winds of hurricanes, typhoons and tornadoes can whip up giant waves. They crash on the shore, smash buildings, flood far inland and cause immense destruction. In 2008, typhoon Nargis hit Burma (Myanmar) in Southeast Asia. It killed more than 200,000 people, made millions homeless, and flooded vast areas with salt water, making the land useless for growing crops.

▼ Tsunamis can flood whole towns along the coast, washing salt water and mud everywhere. Houses were flattened near the coast of Banda Aceh, Indonesia, after a tsunami in 2004.

▲ In the past being a lighthouse-keeper was a vital but lonely job, with weeks alone tending the lamp and its machinery. Today most lighthouses, such as Fanad Head in north-west Ireland, are electric and mostly automatic.

75 For centuries fire beacons, lanterns, lighthouses and lightships have warned boats and ships about dangerous shores. Hazards include running aground on a sandbank or hitting rocks just under the surface. Each lighthouse flashes at a different time interval so sailors can identify it.

▼ The stonefish's fin spines can jab deadly venom into the skin.

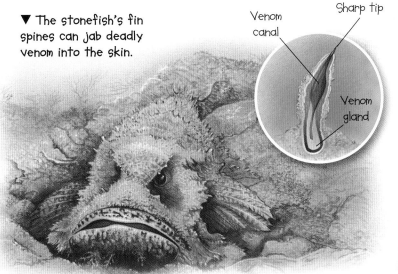

Venom canal

Sharp tip

Venom gland

▼ Fire coral is named after the burning pain it causes if touched.

76 Even just walking along a shore or paddling in shallow water can be dangerous, especially in tropical regions. There may be poisonous animals such as jellyfish, weeverfish, stonefish and shellfish known as coneshells, all of which have stings that can kill.

People and seashores

77 People have lived along seashores and coastlines for thousands of years. Settlers could hunt and gather food from the sea. They could travel by boat along the coast, up rivers to inland areas and across the sea to other regions. These boats carried raw materials, food and goods for trading.

78 Foods from the seashore include fish, octopus, crabs and lobsters caught with nets, spears or hooks and lines. Shellfish such as cockles, mussels, scallops, limpets and winkles are gathered by hand. Seaweeds can be harvested for food or to obtain chemicals used in many processes from dyeing textiles to glass-making.

79 Seashores are important in traditional arts, crafts and religions. Driftwood is carved into fantastic shapes, seashells are collected for their beauty, and necklaces made of sharks' teeth supposedly give strength to the wearer. Gods and spirits from the sea feature in many religions, faiths and customs, such as Kauhuhu the shark god of Hawaii.

▼ Sri Lankan fishermen perch on poles and watch for fish passing below as the tide changes.

▲ Lights never go out in Hong Kong harbour, one of the world's busiest seaports.

▼ More than 150,000 troops landed on Normandy beaches in France on D-Day, 6 June, 1944.

80 In recent times, large areas of coastal land in places such as the Netherlands, India, Bangladesh and southern USA have been made into rich farmlands. Sea walls and other defences keep the waves at bay. Reclaimed land is used for factories and industry, dwellings (as in Venice and Singapore), and airport runways (as in Sydney, Singapore and Hong Kong).

▼ Holiday developments completely destroy natural coasts, with increased travel by air and sea as tourists come and go.

81 Seashores have featured in empires and battles through the ages. Seafaring and trading centres, such as Constantinople (now Istanbul), Venice and London, were once hubs of great empires. Castles and forts keep out seaborne invaders. World War II's D-Day seaborne invasion of France's Normandy coastline in 1944 was the largest military event in history.

Seaside adventures

82 In modern times, seashores have become places for fun, leisure and adventure. People relax, sunbathe, play games and sports, and view buildings and monuments. In many countries, more than half of all tourism business is along coasts.

▲ Scuba-divers should 'take nothing but photographs and memories', leaving wildlife completely untouched.

▼ Adding just the right amount of water makes the sand firm for sculpting.

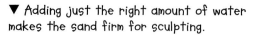

83 Fun activities at the seashore include swimming, snorkelling, scuba-diving, kite-flying and building sandcastles. People also paint, draw and photograph beautiful scenes of the waves, shore, sky and Sun. Many seaside resorts have sand sculpture competitions, where contestants produce amazing shapes from just sand and water.

84 Some seashores attract sportspeople, especially large flat beaches, which can be used by horse riders, runners and racers. Sand racing takes many forms, from land-yachts with wheels blown along by sails, to record-breaking racing cars. Softer sand is best for volleyball, football, bowls and similar ball games.

SAND SCULPTING

You will need:
half a bucket of clean play sand
large tray   small cup   water

Start with dry sand. Pour it onto the tray and try to shape it into a tower or castle. Put it back in the bucket, mix in one cup of water and try again. Then add another cup, try again, and so on. At what stage is the sand best for shaping and sculpting?

85 In shallow water along the shore, people do sports such as surfing, windsurfing, kitesurfing, waterskiing, jetskiing and paragliding. There is also rod fishing, spear fishing, beach netting and other pastimes which could result in a tasty meal.

▼ Bondi Beach near Sydney, Australia, is famous for its surfing and lifesaving displays — but it also gets very crowded.

86 Sea walls and pleasure piers extend from the shore, allowing people to stroll along, do some sea fishing or see a show in the theatre at the end. The longest pleasure pier in the world is Southend Pier in Essex, England, at 2160 metres.

▼ Pleasure piers, such as Southend Pier, were popular in the last century, but few new ones are built.

Trade and power

▶ Modern ports, such as this one in Singapore, are busy day and night all through the year.

87 Cities, ports and industrial centres have been set up along seashores all over the world. There are harbours, docks, wharves and warehouses where cargo ships and passengers come and go, as part of global trade and travel.

88 Today's world uses energy at an increasing rate and many energy sources come through or from seashores. Petroleum (oil) and gas supertankers arrive at coastal storage centres, depots and refineries, where they load or unload their cargoes.

89 Many electricity-generating power stations are along seashores. Big ships can unload supplies of coal, oil, gas and other energy sources directly to them. Another reason is that they can use sea water to cool their generating equipment, to make electricity more efficiently.

▲ At Mossel Bay, South Africa, dozens of giant tanks store natural gas from wells out at sea.

90 Electricity can be generated at seashores, especially from the moving water of tides and waves. The flowing water turns underwater turbine blades connected to generators when the tide comes in and goes out. Wave power is more difficult to harness because big storms can smash the generating equipment.

91 Factories making products are often sited along the coast. Cargo ships bring raw materials, such as coal, oil and metal ores, and take away finished products ranging from MP3 players to giant trucks. Unfortunately, factory wastes and unwanted chemicals may flow or discharge along pipes into the sea.

▲ The Limpet is one type of small wave-power generator being tested in Scotland.

Seashores in trouble

92 Seashores and their animals and plants face all sorts of threats and dangers. Pollution occurs in many forms, such as oil spills, chemical waste from factories, and dirty water and sewage from towns and cities. All kinds of rubbish litters the shore.

▲ In Namibia, Africa, desert comes right to the sea. Many ships have run aground and been wrecked, rusting away along this 'Skeleton Coast'.

I DON'T BELIEVE IT!

Along some busy beaches, more than one in ten particles or grains is not sand – it is plastic. Known as 'beach confetti', this plastic sand is a growing problem worldwide.

93 Seashore tourist centres and holiday resorts may be fun, but they cause big problems. They bring coastal roads, seaports and airports, bright lights, activity and noise to the shore and shallow waters. This frightens away shore creatures such as fish, crabs, seals, sea turtles and birds.

▼ This pile of plastic and other debris in Dorset, England, is typical of the pollution washed up after a storm.

94 Modern shore fishing and food harvesting does immense damage. Powerful boats with huge nets scour and scrape up life from the water and sea bed, leaving them empty. People fish with dynamite and poisonous chemicals. Unique habitats are destroyed and will take years to recover.

▲ Plastic nets and lines do not rot away naturally. They may trap animals, such as this green turtle, for months.

95 Global warming and climate change are looming problems for the whole Earth – especially seashores. Sea levels will rise, altering the shapes of coasts, wiping out natural shore habitats and man-made ones, and flooding low-lying land beyond, from wild areas to cities and rich farmland.

96 With global warming and climate change, more extreme weather may come along coasts. Hurricanes, typhoons and other storms could happen more often, causing destruction along the shores. Today's coastal flood defences, such as sea walls and estuary barriers, will be overwhelmed.

▼ Recycled materials can be used as sea walls to protect against rising sea levels – but they only last a few years.

SOS – Save our seashores

97 **Seashores need our protection and conservation in many ways.** Each shore is a unique habitat, and once gone, it may never return. With problems such as pollution coming from both the land and the sea, seashores are stuck in the middle and need extra care.

▼ Whales sometimes get stranded on beaches, perhaps because they are ill from pollution. Efforts to save them do not always succeed.

98 **One way to conserve seashores is to make them protected nature reserves, wildlife parks or heritage sites.** The area might be protected land that extends to the sea or a marine park that extends to the land. The world's biggest such park, at 360,000 square kilometres, is the Pacific's Papahānaumokuākea Marine National Monument. It includes the northwestern Hawaiian islands and the seas around.

99 You can help to protect seashores by supporting wildlife and conservation organizations, from huge international charities to smaller local ones. In the UK, contact your county-based Wildlife Trust and ask about seashore projects that might need help.

▲ Scientists travel to remote beaches to study wildlife, such as these walruses, and to find out how their seashore habitats are changing.

100 You can even help seashores on your own!

❮ Don't drop litter or leave rubbish along the shore, and ask others not to either.

❮ Encourage people to look after their seashores.

❮ Join an organized beach litter-pick or shore clean-up.

❮ Don't buy souvenirs that might have come from living wildlife, such as dried seahorses and starfish.

❮ Tell someone in authority (police, lifeguard, coastguard) if you come across an injured or stranded animal – but do not touch it.

Index